T0112707

MY FIRST
Swim Class

By Alyssa Satin Capucilli
Photographs by Jill Wachter

Ready-to-Read

Simon Spotlight
New York London Toronto Sydney New Delhi

Never go near or in a pool without your grown-up.

For my friends at the Tarrytown YMCA Aquatics program
who fill the pool with splashes, swimmers, and smiles!
—A.S.C.

To all the little swimmers as they navigate
through the waters of life
—J.W.

SIMON SPOTLIGHT
An imprint of Simon & Schuster Children's Publishing Division
1230 Avenue of the Americas, New York, New York 10020
This Simon Spotlight edition April 2018
Text copyright © 2018 by Alyssa Satin Capucilli
All photographs of adult swim coaches copyright © 2018 by Thinkstock
All other photographs and illustrations copyright © 2018 by Simon & Schuster, Inc.
For information about special discounts for bulk purchases, please contact Simon & Schuster Special Sales at
1-866-506-1949 or business@simonandschuster.com.
Manufactured in the United States of America 0318 LAK
2 4 6 8 10 9 7 5 3 1
Library of Congress Cataloging-in-Publication Data
Names: Capucilli, Alyssa Satin, 1957– author. | Wachter, Jill, photographer.
Title: My first swim class / Alyssa Satin Capucilli ; photographs by Jill Wachter.
Description: First edition. | New York : Simon Spotlight, 2018. | Series: Ready to read | Audience: Age 3–5.
Identifiers: LCCN 2017025852 | ISBN 9781534404878 (paperback) | ISBN 9781534404885 (hc) |
ISBN 9781534404892 (eBook)
Subjects: LCSH: Swimming—Juvenile literature. | BISAC: JUVENILE NONFICTION / Readers / Beginner. |
JUVENILE NONFICTION / Sports & Recreation / General. | JUVENILE NONFICTION / Social Issues /
New Experience.
Classification: LCC GV837.6 .C36 2018 | DDC 797.2/1083—dc23
LC record available at https://lccn.loc.gov/2017025852

It is time for my first swim class.

I am ready to begin.
I have my swim cap,
my goggles, and my suit.

I am ready to swim!

Keeping safe in the water
is our number one rule.

Some classes get special belts
to help us in the pool.

First, we practice kicking.

I try big kicks and small.

We keep our legs straight.

There are splashes for all!

We hold our hands in the air like big round spoons.

We scoop, and we paddle.

It will be pool time soon!

Time to go swimming!
"We are ready!" we shout.

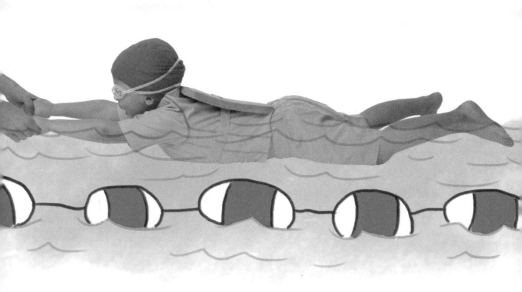

I swim across the pool.

Coach Tan helps me out.

I put my face in the water.

I blow bubbles like a fish.

Blow, blow, blow, blow!

Swish, swish, swish!

We pretend to be starfish.

I try to float on my back.

My arms and legs are wide.

Hooray! I can do that.

We scoop, and we paddle.
We practice kicking and
floating, too.

We can jump into the water,
like leaping frogs do!

SPLASH!

After lots of practice,
we will swim like dolphins
in the sea.

For now we get warm towels.

Swim class is for me!

Do you want to learn to swim?

Find a grown-up to help you practice the swimming strokes in this book, but remember: Never go to a pool unless a grown-up has agreed to keep you safe. Even people who know how to swim need lifeguards!

Let's Get Ready

Are you ready for swim class?

1 Cap and Goggles

A swim cap keeps your hair
out of your face.
Goggles help keep
water out of your eyes.

2 Safety Belt

Some classes may use a safety belt;
others may not. Your instructor
will know just what you need.

3 A Lifeguard

Be sure to wait until a grown-up invites you
into the pool. That's a great and safe pool rule!

Practice

1 Kick Your Legs

Sit on the edge of the pool.
Keep your legs as straight as
railroad tracks.
Choo, choo!

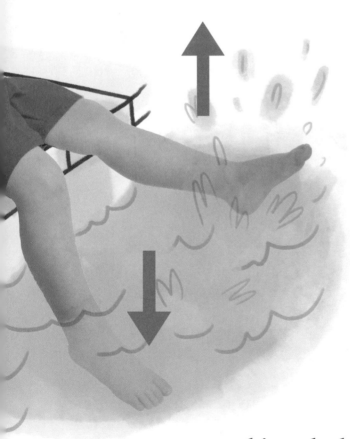

Can you kick and make a big splash?
Try a small splash, too!

2 Scoop and Paddle

Hold your hands in the air.
Curve your fingers so they are
nice and round like a spoon.

Scoop and paddle your
hands through the water.
Great job!

Bubble Time and Back Float

1 Bubble Time

Blow, blow, blow, blow!
Can you blow bubbles like a fish?

Blow, blow, blow, blow!
Can you blow even bigger
bubbles?

2 Back Float

Rest on your back in the water.

Stretch your arms and legs out wide.

Be sure to keep your tummy lifted up to the sky.

Keep your chin up too. Floating is fun!

Let's swim!

1 Wait

Wait until the coach says it is your turn.

2 Start

Once you are in the pool, keep your legs out behind you.

3 Swim

Kick your feet and paddle with your arms.

You did it!

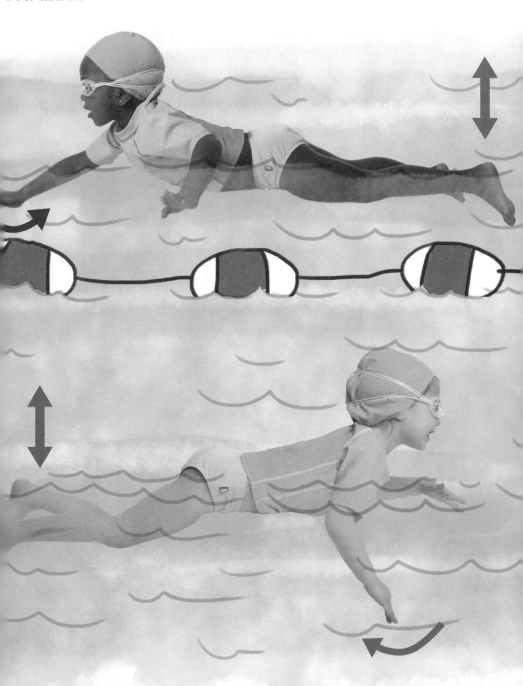

Swim class is fun!

Every time you come to swim class
you will learn something new!
For now, dry off with a warm towel and give
your teacher a high five.

You did it! You are learning to swim.